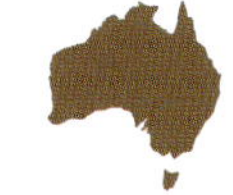

AUSTRALIAN LANDSCAPES

MOUNTAINS

IN AUSTRALIA

RACHEL DIXON

REDBACK publishing

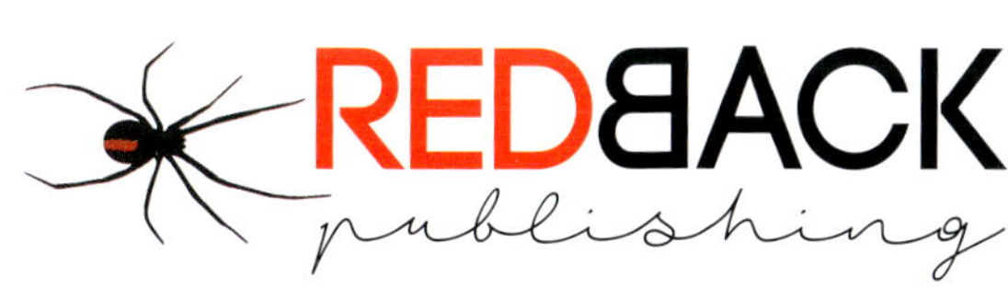

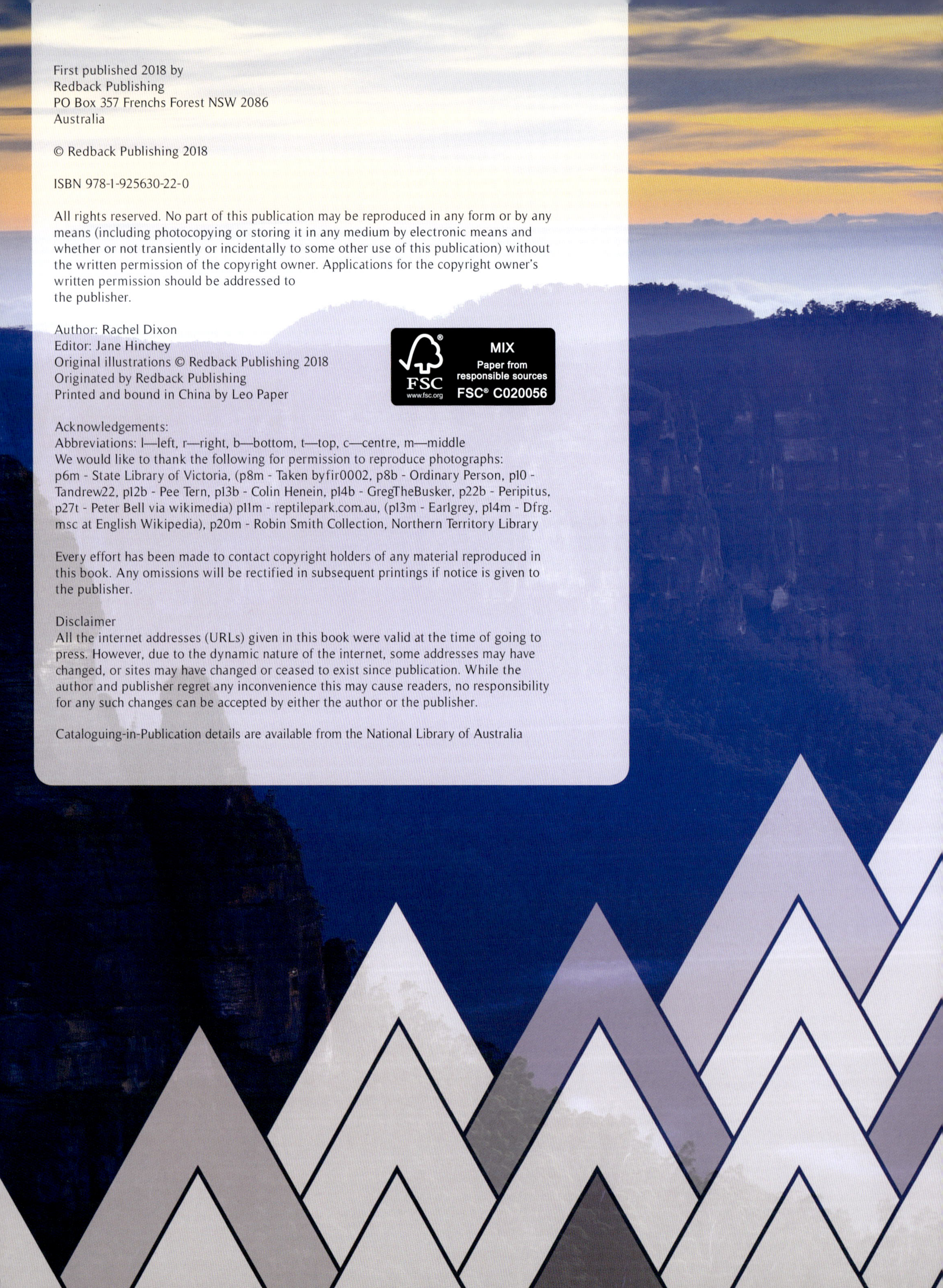

First published 2018 by
Redback Publishing
PO Box 357 Frenchs Forest NSW 2086
Australia

ISBN 978-1-925630-22-0

Author: Rachel Dixon
Editor: Jane Hinchey
Original illustrations © Redback Publishing 2018
Originated by Redback Publishing
Printed and bound in China by Leo Paper

Acknowledgements:
Abbreviations: l—left, r—right, b—bottom, t—top, c—centre, m—middle
We would like to thank the following for permission to reproduce photographs:
p6m - State Library of Victoria, (p8m - Taken byfir0002, p8b - Ordinary Person, p10 - Tandrew22, p12b - Pee Tern, p13b - Colin Henein, p14b - GregTheBusker, p22b - Peripitus, p27t - Peter Bell via wikimedia) p11m - reptilepark.com.au, (p13m - Earlgrey, p14m - Dfrg.msc at English Wikipedia), p20m - Robin Smith Collection, Northern Territory Library

Cataloguing-in-Publication details are available from the National Library of Australia

Contents

Mountain Building in Australia

Australia's mountains are not high by world standards, but they have influenced the spread of human settlement, and still affect the weather and the presence of water in the environment.

Mountains are formed when the earth's tectonic plates collide or slide across each other and rock layers are lifted or folded. These underground forces can also cause rock layers to split apart, resulting in huge blocks of rock falling or being pushed upwards. The tectonic plate on which Australia sits is moving north at a rate of about seven centimetres a year. Australia also has ancient, inland plains where there has been no mountain-building activity for millions of years.

Although there is no major volcanic activity happening on the mainland of Australia now, active volcanoes have left their mark on the landscape. These volcanoes cooled over thousands of years and are now extinct. When they erupted, heated magma came up to the surface, spilling out as lava. The volcanoes that formed in this way do not erupt now as they are no longer connected beneath the ground to a source of hot magma.

Right: Mount Dromedary, J. Lycett 1824

Mountains and Aboriginal Australians

Australian Aboriginal Dreamtime stories are a rich resource that details the history of mountains. The Rainbow Serpent, ancestor spirits and spirits of the earth, land and sky have all had a role in creating the mountains across the land.

The features of each mountain have been left as signs for the Aboriginal custodians to remind them of their ancestors and the duty they have to care for their lands. Other people who visit mountainous regions of Australia need to be aware that they may be treading on or driving across spiritual sites and behave with respect.

CASE STUDY

Mount Dromedary in New South Wales is an extinct volcano and it was once mined for gold, both in surface streams and by digging tunnels into the mountain. In 2006, Mount Dromedary was handed back to its traditional custodians, the Yuin people, whose name for it is Gulaga. The mountain is a sacred site where women would go to perform ceremonies and to give birth. Gulaga is a Dreamtime mother and her two sons have stayed near her as an island and as a smaller hill.

Mountains and Settlers in Australia

Exploration

- The Great Dividing Range on the east coast was a barrier to further settlement inland until explorers found a way across it.
- Explorers wrote about the depressing flat plains of inland Australia and felt the need to be the first to climb any mountains or high rocks they found.
- Mountains provided reference points for explorers looking for ways to record their location.

Water

- When high mountains intercept moisture-laden air, the water condenses out of the atmosphere and falls as rain or snow. Mountains are the source of many rivers and are responsible for carrying rainwater down into drier regions.
- When snow melts on mountain tops, high-energy rivers are produced. The water from these rivers powers the turbines of hydroelectricity generators.

Wonnangatta Station; Great Dividing Range, 1935

The Arts

- Mountains have inspired many Australian artists, including Albert Namatjira and a number of colonial artists. Mountains also feature in literature by writers such as Joan Lindsay. Her novel Picnic at Hanging Rock was set in the Macedon Ranges of Victoria.

Transport

- The building of roads and mass transport systems, like railways, is difficult and sometimes even impossible in mountainous areas.

Bushfires

- Because access roads are often limited in mountainous areas, escape during a bushfire can be difficult. Bushfires tend to sweep up hillsides, so this produces an additional hazard for people who live in the bush on mountainsides.

Timber

- Timber was an important resource for early settlers. The difficulty of logging on steep mountainsides has protected some of these environments from deforestation and erosion.

Mountains and the Economy in Australia

Tourism

- Tourists visiting mountainous regions support local businesses, which contributes to employment.
  - **Skiing**: The ski industry in Australia requires extensive infrastructure to operate in extreme winter conditions. Alpine areas are now important sites for snow tourism and snow sports.
  - **Ecotourism**: Tourists visit ecotourism developments in mountains to experience the natural surroundings.

Above: Perisher snowfields

Mining

- Mountains across Australia are mined for a variety of products, including metal ores and coal. Mountain ranges that formed when layers of rock were twisted and uplifted provide miners with easier access to ore bearing deposits.

Real Estate

- The release of building sites in mountainous areas contributes to the building industry. House buyers place a high value on panoramic mountain views.

Livestock Grazing and Agriculture

- The grasslands on the high plateaus in Australia's mountainous areas are used for livestock grazing during the warmer months of the year. The mountain tablelands also provide high rainfall areas for agriculture.

Great Dividing Range

The Great Dividing Range is the longest mountain range in Australia, and is known by many different names along its course. It extends from Cape York in northern Queensland, and runs down eastern Australia to the Grampians in Victoria. A part of the range also extends beneath Bass Strait and comes to the surface again in Tasmania, where it forms the high country in the centre of that state.

The range consists of mountains as well as hills and high, flat areas called tablelands and plateaus. The alpine regions of Australia, as well as the high plateaus forming the Darling Downs in Queensland, are all part of this one mountain range.

Millions of years ago, geologic activity deep beneath the surface resulted in the folding and uplifting of the rocks of the Great Dividing Range. Before this event, the area was a flat seabed. Fossils of shells found in rocks at the tops of mountains are from those times.

Businesses that quarry the coloured sandstone of the Great Dividing Range are making use of the rocks that were formed when ancient rivers deposited sand. Heat and pressure then converted this into sandstone.

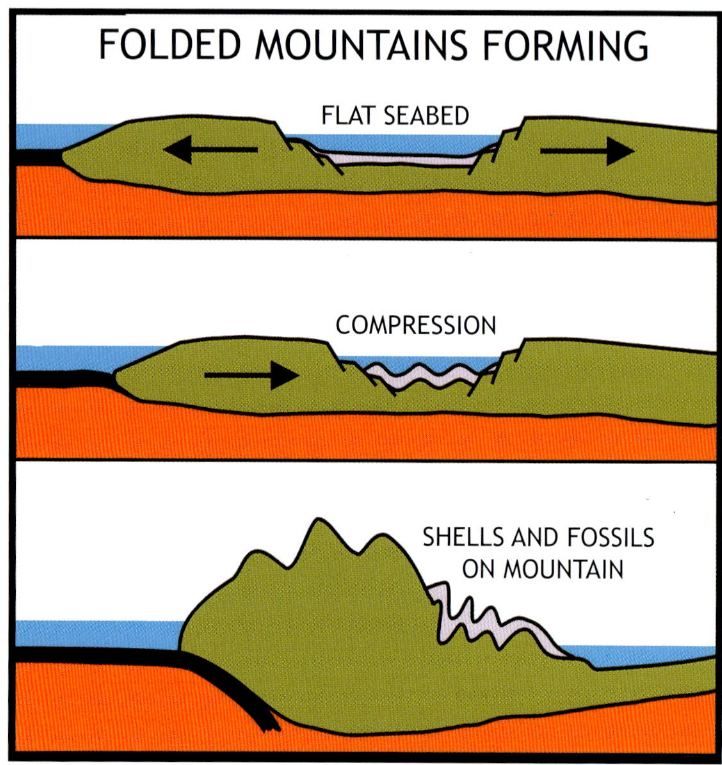

The range contributes to the dryness of the plains in the west as it stops moisture-laden air reaching them from the east. Tributaries of the Murray River rise on the western slopes. The Snowy River, which feeds the Snowy Mountains Hydro-electric Scheme, rises on the eastern slopes. As the source of so many rivers, the Great Dividing Range is vital to the water supply of the lowlands on both sides of it.

Early settlers were confined to the east coast until they found a way to cross The Great Dividing Range through a pass at the Blue Mountains near Sydney. The colony's need for more land for agriculture and for grazing livestock was a driving force in the history of mountain exploration in Australia.

Right: Yarrunga Valley, Great Dividing Range

Australian Alps

The Australian Alps include mountain ranges in the Australian Capital Territory, New South Wales and Victoria. They are a part of the Great Dividing Range and include a variety of environments. The tops of the mountains are alpine, with low bushes and mosses that are covered with snow during the winter. Snow also sometimes falls at other times of the year. Further down is the sub-alpine region, where trees can grow. The tablelands of the Australian Alps are flat areas with a high altitude.

Livestock Grazing

Scattered throughout the Australian Alps are the remains of stockmen's huts that were built when farmers took cattle into the alpine areas for summer grazing and then moved them to lower altitudes for the winter.

Mining

The gold rush in the Australian Alps brought thousands of people to the area. Silver and tin were also mined in the Kosciuszko National Park until the 1930s.

Forestry

State forests occupy a small part of the Australian Alps producing timber for commercial use.

FAST FACT

If the weather in winter is not cold enough, the mountain pygmy possum will wake from its hibernation at a time when there is no food available for it.

Australian Alpine Wildlife

Plants

Alpine bogs - Bogs are areas with low shrubs and mosses that store water and gradually release it. The water forms rivulets that eventually flow into rivers.

Alpine trees - Trees only grow below the tree line and include mountain ash, swamp gums, blue gums and snow gums.

Flowering plants - These include marigolds that start to flower under the snow, native buttercups and snow daisies.

Grasses - Grasses and bushes dominate the alpine tablelands. Farmers use the grasslands for grazing livestock.

Animals

Alpine dingoes - Dingoes that live in alpine areas have thick fur to keep them warm.

Wild brumbies - Although brumbies are feral horses, their representation in Australian songs, poems and literature has resulted in them becoming symbols of the alpine regions. They appear on Australia's ten dollar note illustrating the poem The Man From Snowy River by Banjo Paterson.

Mountain birds - Some of these birds migrate within the same region, retreating to lower altitudes when snow covers the mountain tops. The gang-gang cockatoo stays in the sub-alpine forests, even when snow falls.

Corroboree frog - This frog has distinctive black and gold markings and lives in alpine marshes.

CASE STUDY

Mountain Pygmy Possum

The mountain pygmy possum is the only marsupial animal in Australia that hibernates during the winter. These tiny, exquisite possums find holes amongst the boulders on the ground to live in. They rely on the annual migration of Bogong moths into the mountains and feast on them to build up their resources for the winter hibernation. The moths hide in the boulders as well, making them an easy food source for the pygmy possum to find.

The mountain pygmy possum is an endangered species and is under threat from:

- destruction of its habitat
- feral cats
- anything that reduces the Bogong moth population
- global warming

Regions in the Australian Alps

1. Snowy Mountains - NSW
2. Brindabella Range - ACT and NSW
3. Victorian Alps - VIC

1. Snowy Mountains

In New South Wales, the Australian Alps are called the Snowy Mountains. The Kosciuszko National Park covers most of this alpine region.

The Snowy Mountains are the location of the Snowy Mountains Hydro-electric Scheme and of Mount Kosciuszko.

Mount Kosciuszko

Mount Kosciuszko is the highest mountain in Australia at 2,228 metres high. Paul Edmund Strzelecki, the Polish explorer, named it in 1840.

Visitors can walk to the summit during the warmer months of the year, but there is also a chairlift. In winter it is covered in snow and the weather can produce extreme conditions. Lake Cootapatamba, the highest lake in Australia, lies just below the summit.

Snowy Mountains Scheme

The Snowy Mountains Hydro-electric Scheme is one of the most impressive civil engineering projects ever undertaken anywhere worldwide. Sixteen dams, 145 kilometres of tunnels, hundreds of kilometres of piping, a pumping station and nine power stations were constructed between 1949 and 1974. More than 100,000 people came from over thirty countries to work on the project.

2. Brindabella Range

The Brindabella Range section of the Australian Alps begins in the Australian Capital Territory and extends across the border to New South Wales. The Namadgi National Park and the Brindabella National Park are in this mountain range. The area provides many tracks for 4WD enthusiasts.

Australian Alps Walking Track

For bushwalkers who want to see everything the Australian Alps have to offer, there is a 65 kilometre track that follows the mountain ridges. There are basic mountain huts along the way where walkers can spend the night. The track extends from Walhalla in Victoria to Tharwa near Canberra.

Above: Mount Ginini - Namadgi National Park

The highest mountain in this range is Bimberi Peak. Although it is not a difficult climb for hikers, the peak is covered in snow in winter and the weather can be unpredictable.

The gold rush brought miners to the Brindabella in the mid 1800s and prospectors still pan for gold in the mountain rivers.

Below: Canberra looking towards the Brindabella Range

3. Victorian Alps

The Victorian Alps are part of the Great Dividing Range and the Australian Alps. Mount Bogong, the highest mountain in Victoria, is in this mountain range. The Victorian Alps is also known as the High Country and is a recreational destination for people seeking to enjoy the snow in winter and bushwalking in the warmer months. The granite cliffs of Mount Buffalo are popular with rock climbers. Below the tree line there are sub-alpine forests, and agricultural land that produces some of Victoria's finest wines. The Alpine National Park is the largest national park in Victoria.

Mining

In 2003, bushfires devastated large parts of the Victorian Alps. After the fire had burned away the bush, ruins of abandoned gold mines revealed the harsh and isolated conditions that early gold miners experienced. In the 1990s, copper was also mined in the Victorian Alps.

Cattle Grazing

Cattle grazing in the Alpine National Park continued until 2015 when the Victorian government legislated to ban it. Cattle farmers and conservationists continue to disagree about the damage that grazing causes and whether grazing is beneficial because it may reduce bushfire risk by removing undergrowth.

What is the Tree Line?

Australian native trees cannot grow on mountains where the temperature is too low for them. This results in the tree line, which is where trees stop growing. Beyond the tree line there are only alpine shrubs.

Left: early autumn snowfall Mount Bogong Below: Mount Bogong

Snow Sports in Australia

Although most tourists associate Australia with red deserts and beaches, there is also a thriving snow tourism industry in the alpine regions. Snow tourism provides employment and is a boost to the economy of towns around the snowfields in New South Wales, Victoria and Tasmania.

Above: Kiandra

History of Snow Sports in Australia

Kiandra in New South Wales is the location of Australia's first ski club, formed in 1861. Skiing increased in popularity after the 1950s, when migrants from Europe came to Australia.

Winter Olympics and Australia's Alpine Regions

The Australian ski fields have inspired a number of young athletes to strive to reach a standard that would allow them to compete at the Winter Olympics. Australians have competed in every Winter Olympics since 1936, except for those held in St Moritz in 1948. In the 1990s, Australia's performance improved after the creation of the Olympic Winter Institute of Australia and the purchase of a training base in Austria. The first gold medals were won in 2002.

Above: Two-man bobsleigh heat in Sochi, Russia 2014

New South Wales

The largest ski resorts in New South Wales are located at Jindabyne, Perisher, Charlotte Pass, Mount Selwyn and Thredbo. Mount Kosciuszko is popular with bushwalkers and a track leads to the summit.

Victoria

Popular ski resorts in Victoria are located at Mount Buller, Mount Hotham and Falls Creek in the Alpine National Park.

Tasmania

Ski slopes in Ben Lomond National Park or at Mount Mawson are a short drive from city centres, making them an easy destination for people from Hobart and Launceston.

Bushwalking along the Overland Track in the Lake St Clair National Park attracts walkers who want a challenge. Snow and ice can make trekking conditions extreme during the winter. The track takes six days to complete and huts are provided along the route for refuge.

Alpine Tourism and the Environment

- Bushwalking through the alpine areas attracts walkers who enjoy a challenging trek through highlands.

- Special building methods need to take into account avalanches and the build-up of melt water in spring.

- Tourists who visit alpine regions to experience the natural environment are also contributing to its degradation. There needs to be a balance between keeping the alpine areas pristine and catering for tourists who want to visit them.

- The snow tourism industry will be threatened if climate change causes a rise in temperature.

- The snow tourism industry needs to manage the environment to exist. Ski runs are cleared of trees and smoothed, and infrastructure such as ski lifts, buildings, roads, railways and sewerage systems all need to be built to look after the tourists. As ski resorts become more popular, more land has to be claimed for further building.

Below: Perisher Valley

Volcanic Mountains in Australia

Active Volcanoes

There are no active volcanoes on the Australian mainland, but there are two active volcanoes on islands in the southern ocean. Big Ben volcano on Heard Island erupted in 2016 sending lava out onto the snow. The highest point of the Big Ben volcano is Mawson Peak, named after the Antarctic explorer, Douglas Mawson.

The second active Australian volcano is on the McDonald Islands in the southern ocean. There are other active volcanoes on the sea floor in the subarctic region. These play a role in the ocean currents and the release of chemicals into the water,

Extinct Volcanoes

Researchers at the Australian National University have only recently identified an ancient volcanic chain of mountains. This mountain range runs all the way from Cape Hillsborough on the Queensland coast down to Victoria.

Mount Gambier in South Australia is a volcano that is no longer active, although it may have erupted as recently as 5,000 years ago. The Blue Lake was formed as part of this volcanic activity. Mount Schank is another ancient volcano a short distance away. It erupted only a few thousand years ago and Australian Aboriginal Dreaming stories suggest the local people witnessed this event.

Mount Warning is an ancient volcano in New South Wales. It erupted millions of years ago.

The Kanawinka Global Geopark is Australia's only region based on volcanic activity. Covering areas from South Australia to Victoria, the Geopark includes the sites of over sixty volcanoes and hundreds of places where lava once flowed onto the surface.

Scientists are still discovering extinct and active volcanoes on the sea floor around Australia.

Below: Blue Lake Mount Gambier

Right: Mount Warning Far right: Path on Mount Warning trail

MacDonnell Ranges, Northern Territory

The MacDonnell Ranges are rocky, low mountains that stretch for 600 kilometres in the Northern Territory, with Alice Springs sited in a gap in the middle. Parts of these ranges are in the Tjoritja / West MacDonnell National Park. The red mountains have gorges, waterfalls and rock crevices. There are also hidden springs with lush vegetation growing in the midst of the desert, and wildlife that depends on the protection of the rocky habitat and the microclimates that the MacDonnell Ranges provide. Palm Valley contains rare plants that are remnants from a time when the whole region was much wetter and palms and ferns could flourish. Mount Zeil, at about 1,500 metres high, is the tallest peak in these ranges and in the Northern Territory.

Australian Aboriginal People and the MacDonnell Ranges

There is an ochre mining site in the mountains that was used by generations of Aboriginal people. They mined the red, yellow and white ochre for ceremonial purposes and also traded it with other groups. The rocks walls and caves are the locations of many examples of Aboriginal rock art. Emily Gap and Jessie Gap in the eastern part of the ranges are part of the Yeperenye caterpillar Dreaming trail of the Arrernte people.

Below: MacDonnell Ranges Right: Ochre pit

Rare Wildlife of the MacDonnell Ranges

- Black-footed wallabies
- MacDonnell Ranges cycad
- Red cabbage palms in Palm Valley

MacDonnell Ranges and the Economy

- **Tourism**

  Tourists use Alice Springs as their base for trips to the MacDonnell Ranges, using local tour operators and accommodation providers. The Ellery Creek Big Hole is a deep waterhole and a popular place for swimming. The Larapinta Trail is a 220 kilometre long tourist route through the ranges.

Left: Red cabbage palms in Palm Valley

Above: The Ellery Creek Big Hole   Right: Arltunga

- **Mining**

  Arltunga is now a ghost town but it was the base for miners after gold was found there in the 1890s. The government was persuaded to establish the Government Battery and Cyanide works at Artlunga in 1896 to keep the town alive, but the harsh conditions, lack of water and unprofitable reserves of gold meant that the town lost its battle for survival.

Flinders Ranges, South Australia

The Flinders Ranges were created 800 million years ago when a seabed lifted. They are the largest mountain range in South Australia.

Wilpena Pound in the Flinders Ranges is a massive depression in the landscape, surrounded by a rim of eroded rocks. It is seventeen kilometres long and St Mary Peak is the highest of the surrounding hills.

The Dreamtime story for Wilpena Pound describes two giant snakes that formed the feature. The Adnyamathanha people ask that visitors do not climb this peak because of its cultural significance. It represents the head of one of these snakes. Early settlers used Wilpena Pound for horse breeding and farming but it is now part of the Flinders Ranges National Park.

Below: Wilpena Pound Bottom left: Southern end of Wilpena Pound

Hamersley Range, Western Australia

These mountains extend across the northwest of Western Australia to the coast and the Indian Ocean. Mount Meharry, the highest mountain in Western Australia, is located in the Hamersley Range. The surrounding animals and plants are all protected by the Karijini National Park, where masses of flowering desert plants bloom after rain and waterfalls spill into mountain gorges.

Mining

Known for its rich iron ore deposits, the Hamersley Range has been the source of most of Australia's iron ore production. Part of the range has been named Hancock Range after Lang Hancock and the Hancock family, who were responsible for developing the iron ore mining industry in Western Australia.

Below: Iron ore mine Right: Karijini National Park

Macedon Ranges, Victoria

The Macedon Ranges were formed millions of years ago from lava flows. They are close to Melbourne, making them a popular tourist destination. In 1836, Captain Hepburn found and named the Hepburn Mineral Spring. The hot mineral springs have drawn people to the area since the 1800s.

Below: view from the Hanging Rocks rock formation in the Macedon Ranges

Dandenong Ranges, Victoria

The low hills of the Dandenong Ranges are home to a wide range of wildlife. Since the late 1800s, the picnic areas and walking trails of the Dandenongs have been welcoming visitors from Melbourne wanting to escape the city. Accommodation in historic hotels, shops selling local arts, crafts and produce, or a ride on the Puffing Billy steam train are just a few of the many attractions.

Below: Puffing Billy steam train   Right: Dandenong Ranges

Mountains in Tasmania

Tasmania is a mountainous island, with over one hundred peaks. The mountains contribute to the hydroelectricity industry in the state and have also been the location of mining ventures.

Mount Wellington

Close to the capital city of Hobart, Mount Wellington forms the picturesque background for much of the promotional material for the city.

Cradle Mountain - Cradle Mountain is in the Lake St Clair National Park. The Overland Track for bushwalkers starts at this mountain and takes six days to complete.

Mount Ossa - The highest mountain in Tasmania.

Mount Lyell - The site of a former copper mine that operated for a century.

Left: Mount Wellington   Below: Cradle Mountain

Mountains in Queensland

Glass House Mountains

The eleven volcanic peaks of the Glass House Mountains were formed when molten rock rose to the surface. The surroundings were eroded away over millions of years, leaving only the hard domes behind. James Cook named them in 1770.

Mount Bartle Frere - The highest mountain in Queensland, located near the northern end of the Great Dividing Range. Tropical rainforest covers the lower slopes. Despite being so far north, the temperature at the top can be cool, so climbers need to be prepared for changes in the weather as they reach the summit.

Bunya Mountains - Located in southern Queensland, these mountains have the largest bunya pine forests in Australia. These forests were once the location of large meetings of Australian Aboriginal people who gathered when the bunya nuts were ready for gathering.

Above: Mount Bartle Frere Below: Glass House Mountains

Blue Mountains, New South Wales

The Blue Mountains, just west of Sydney, have a reputation as a haunt for artists and conservationists. The beautiful scenery throughout the mountains attracts tourists for bushwalking in the summer and for the snow in the winter. The Winter Magic Festival is held each year to celebrate the winter solstice.

Jenolan Caves

Millions of years ago, before the whole area was lifted into mountains, the Jenolan Caves were once part of a seabed. Shell and coral fossils are found in the rocks of the caves, which are Australia's most remarkable limestone cave system.

The traditional owners of the land at Jenolan are the Wiradjuri and the Gundungurra peoples, while the caves are in the lands of the Burra Burra people, a clan group of the Gundungurra Nation. The caves, called Binoomea, were places of ceremonial importance and the cave pools were known for their healing properties.

Settlers discovered the caves in the early 1800s. The damage that some early tourists caused was halted in 1872 when breaking off pieces from the caves was made illegal. In the late 1880s, the Jenolan Caves increased in popularity as a tourist destination.

Left and below: Jenolan Caves

Exploration

The Blue Mountains were the first mountain range explored by settlers. Until they found a way to cross the Blue Mountains to the west of Sydney, they had no idea there were extensive plains suitable for pastures and crops, and large river systems for irrigation. The growing settlement needed more land, so Governor Macquarie encouraged explorers to find out what was over the mountains.

In 1813, Blaxland, Lawson and Wentworth discovered a way across the mountains, allowing settlers to spread into the plains beyond. Aboriginal people had been crossing the Blue Mountains for generations, so the explorers used Aboriginal guides to lead the way. The exploration party followed the ridges of the hills, rather than descending into the valleys, where bushwalkers still lose their way in the dense forests.

Geology

The Blue Mountains are a part of the Great Dividing Range. They were formed by sedimentation, uplifting and twisting of the rock layers and erosion by rivers.

Above: Blue Mountains Top right: The Three Sisters

Three Sisters

The Three Sisters rock formation at Katoomba is one of Australia's most famous landmarks. An extensive infrastructure has been built to allow viewing from a large platform, and to cater for the needs of tourists and their vehicles. A number of local businesses depend on the Three Sisters for their livelihood.

World Heritage Site

The Greater Blue Mountains area has been a UNESCO Word Heritage Site since 2000. The vegetation is important for its connection to the ancient continent of Gondwana. The extensive variety of eucalypt trees is unique and the rare Wollemi pine is a relic from the age of the dinosaurs.

Rock Outcrops

Uluru and Mount Augustus are large rocks that sit in flat desert plains. They are both just the tips of huge masses of rock that are still underground.

Uluru, Northern Territory

Uluru is a single rock, or monolith, that has been exposed by weathering of the surrounding desert. It is over 300 metres high, measures more than nine kilometres around the base and is thought to extend two kilometres underground.

The Pitjantjatjara and Yankunytjatjara (Anangu) Aboriginal people are the traditional custodians of Uluru and Kata Tjuta. The magnificent rock formations represent the lives and works of the creation ancestors and spirits. The first European to find Uluru was William Gosse in 1873. He named it Ayers Rock.

As a ceremonial site for the traditional owners, Uluru has spiritual significance. Tourists are not officially prohibited from climbing Uluru, but the local Yankunytjatjara and Pitjantjatjara people feel that doing this is a desecration. To accommodate the thousands of tourists who come to see and experience Uluru, the village of Yulara was created nearby.

Below: Ayers Rock

Above: Mount Augustus

Mount Augustus, Western Australia

Like Uluru, Mount Augustus is a large rock that rises above a flat plain. Its geologic history is different from that of Uluru as it was formed over a billion years ago when ancient rock layers were uplifted and twisted. At eight kilometres long, it is larger than Uluru and made up of a mixture of rock types.

The Wajarri people's name for this rock is Burringurrah and there are many examples of their rock art in the area.

In 1858, Francis Gregory became the first European to see and climb Mount Augustus, which he named after his brother.

Below: Rock art at Mount Augustus

Glossary

alpine	relating to high, cold mountains
altitude	height above sea level
deforestation	removal of forest trees
desecration	ruination of a sacred place
exquisite	very beautiful and special
extinct volcano	volcano which has not erupted for 10,000 years
lava	molten rock that is expelled onto the surface of the Earth
livelihood	way of earning an income
magma	molten rock underground
microclimate	climatic conditions that exist only in a very restricted location
plateaus	flat areas of land at a high altitude
pristine	very clean and natural
tectonic plates	moving sections of the Earth's crust
uplift	geologic event which creates mountains
winter solstice	shortest day of the year

Index